St. Patrick

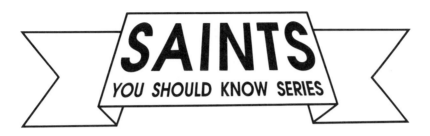

St. Patrick

Margaret and
Matthew Bunson

Our Sunday Visitor Publishing Division
Our Sunday Visitor, Inc.
Huntington, Indiana 46750

ISBN: 0-87973-785-9 (hardcover)
ISBN: 0-87973-559-7 (softcover)
LCCCN: 92-61547

PRINTED IN THE UNITED STATES OF AMERICA

Cover and text illustrations by Margaret Bunson

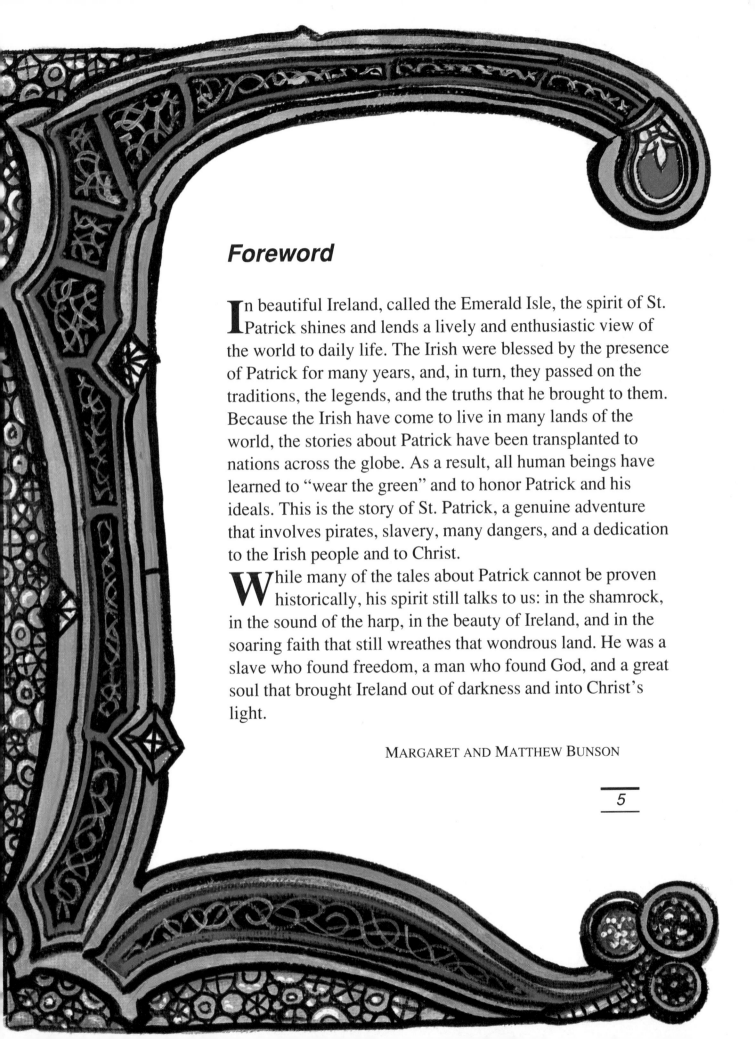

Foreword

In beautiful Ireland, called the Emerald Isle, the spirit of St. Patrick shines and lends a lively and enthusiastic view of the world to daily life. The Irish were blessed by the presence of Patrick for many years, and, in turn, they passed on the traditions, the legends, and the truths that he brought to them. Because the Irish have come to live in many lands of the world, the stories about Patrick have been transplanted to nations across the globe. As a result, all human beings have learned to "wear the green" and to honor Patrick and his ideals. This is the story of St. Patrick, a genuine adventure that involves pirates, slavery, many dangers, and a dedication to the Irish people and to Christ.

While many of the tales about Patrick cannot be proven historically, his spirit still talks to us: in the shamrock, in the sound of the harp, in the beauty of Ireland, and in the soaring faith that still wreathes that wondrous land. He was a slave who found freedom, a man who found God, and a great soul that brought Ireland out of darkness and into Christ's light.

MARGARET AND MATTHEW BUNSON

Every March seventeenth, in cities all over the world, men and women become Irish for the day. No matter who they are or what their nationality happens to be, people wear green, toast the lovely Emerald Isle, and salute a saint who lived around sixteen hundred years ago. In one city the people even dye a very large river green for the celebration.

This much-loved saint is Patrick, a true friend of God who still manages to keep Irish eyes smiling and the hearts of people everywhere beating to the sounds of the pipes and the drums.

There are some historical documents still available that give details about the life of St. Patrick, including two that he wrote himself. Most of what we now know, however, comes from what is called the "oral tradition," stories that one generation after another told around the campfires. Not only were there tales about Patrick, but certain places in Ireland were honored because the saint worked there. The Irish, migrating to countries all across the earth, brought the "oral tradition" about Patrick with them, and his life touched something deep inside human beings, turning his feast day into an international time of laughter and good will.

What was it about Patrick that moves people centuries after his death? What is it about Ireland that makes men and women sigh and linger over maps and photographs of green hills and dales? It is Patrick and his adopted land that shine in the hearts of people everywhere.

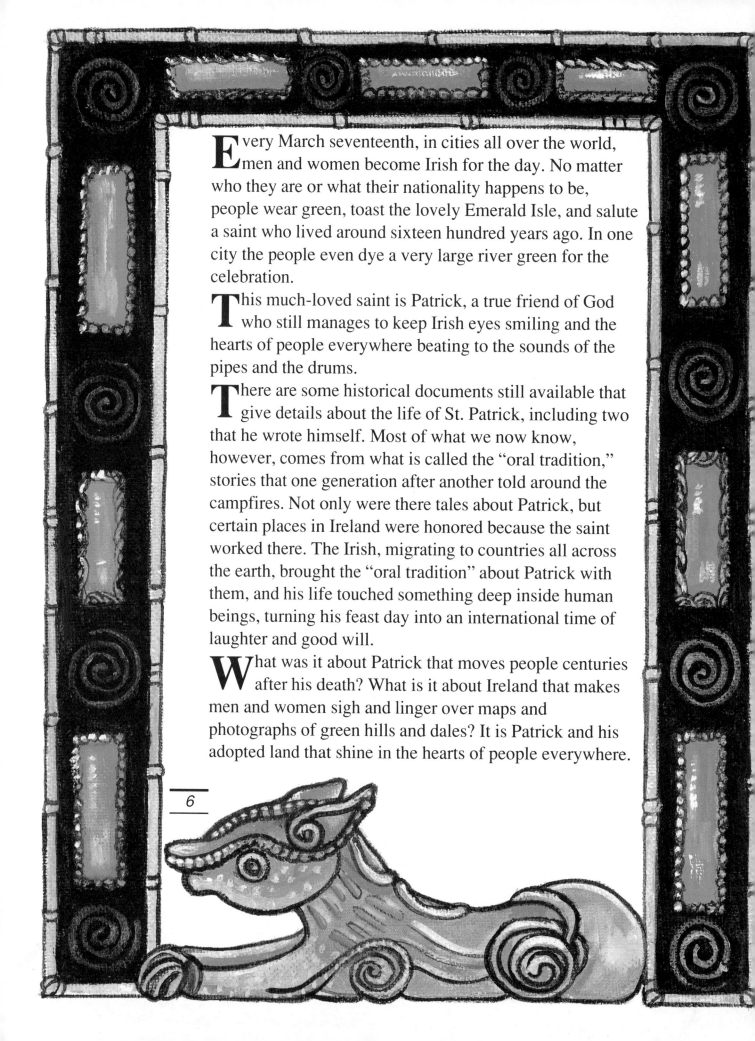

In Ireland — which is also called Eire, Erin, or the Emerald Isle — the high kings ruled. The nation was never conquered by Rome, a power in the first centuries of the Christian era that could unleash thousands of trained soldiers and war machines against lesser lands. Stories about Julius Caesar, Augustus, Nero, and crazy Caligula still interest people. They were part of Rome, which is now called the Eternal City and houses the Vatican, the residence of the Pope. While Ireland was never conquered by Rome, the people on the island — made up of Celts, with some Picts (an ancient tribe of the area) — had great respect for all things Roman. There were Roman forts and towns in Britain, and many areas copied their laws and government.

The *ardris* — the high kings of Ireland — lived in Tara and worked with lesser chiefs and kings to rule over a great culture. The Romans called them barbarians, but the Irish had music, art, silver and metal wares, and skills with ships and weapons. The high kings were brave warriors who sent their raiding ships against the trading vessels of other lands. This custom, called piracy, would bring Patrick to Ireland in time, as it would lead to the coming of the Christian faith to Erin.

Patrick was a Roman citizen of Britain, born into a family of a particular social class. The Romans liked to have everyone know where each of them stood as far as rank and power were concerned. Their society had classes, groups that were born with titles or without them, with wealth or poverty. Few Romans could raise themselves up to a higher social class, and they lived well aware of who they were in the Empire.

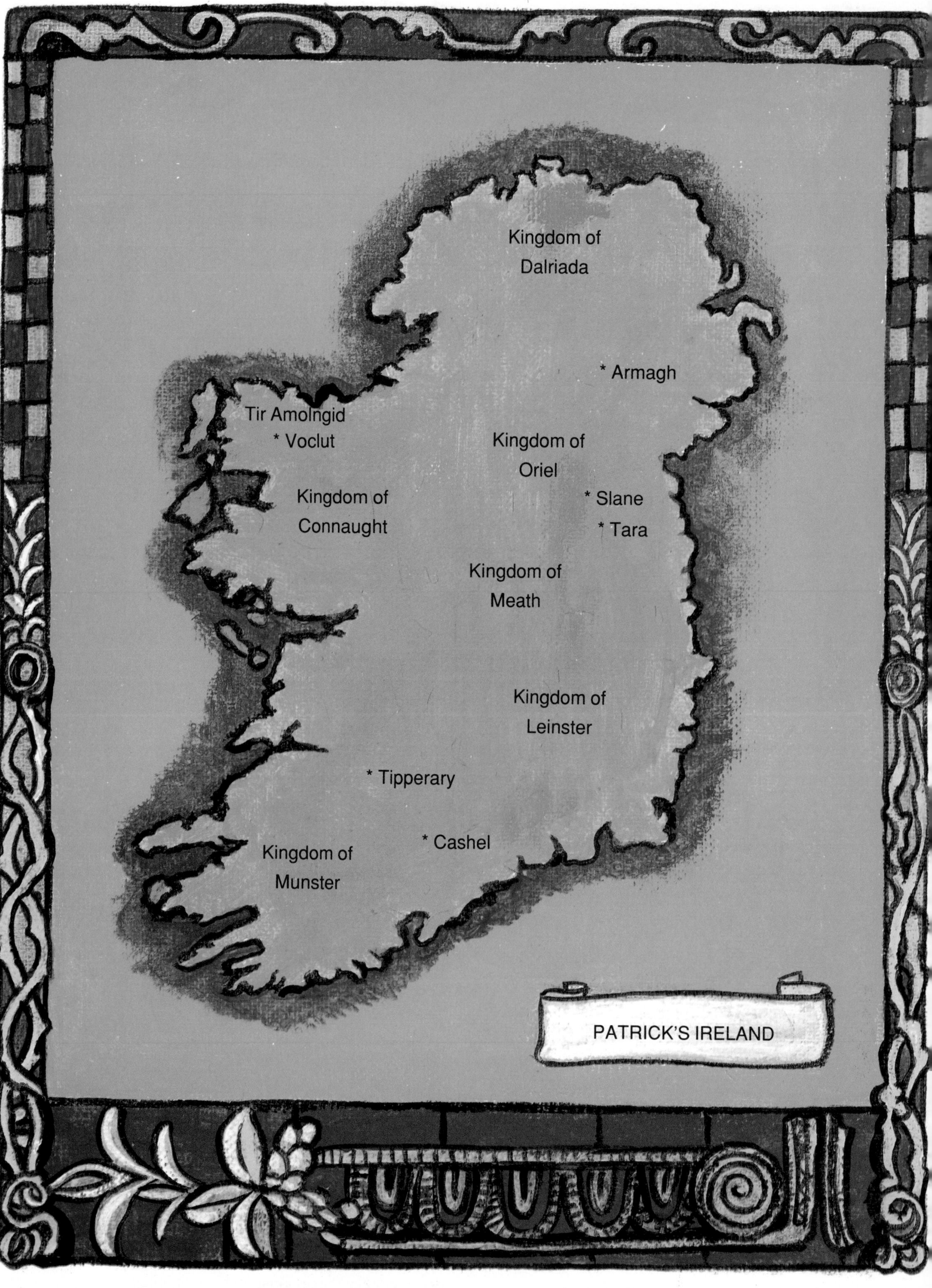

Kingdom of
Dalriada

* Armagh

Tir Amolngid
* Voclut

Kingdom of
Oriel

Kingdom of
Connaught

* Slane
* Tara

Kingdom of
Meath

Kingdom of
Leinster

* Tipperary

* Cashel

Kingdom of
Munster

PATRICK'S IRELAND

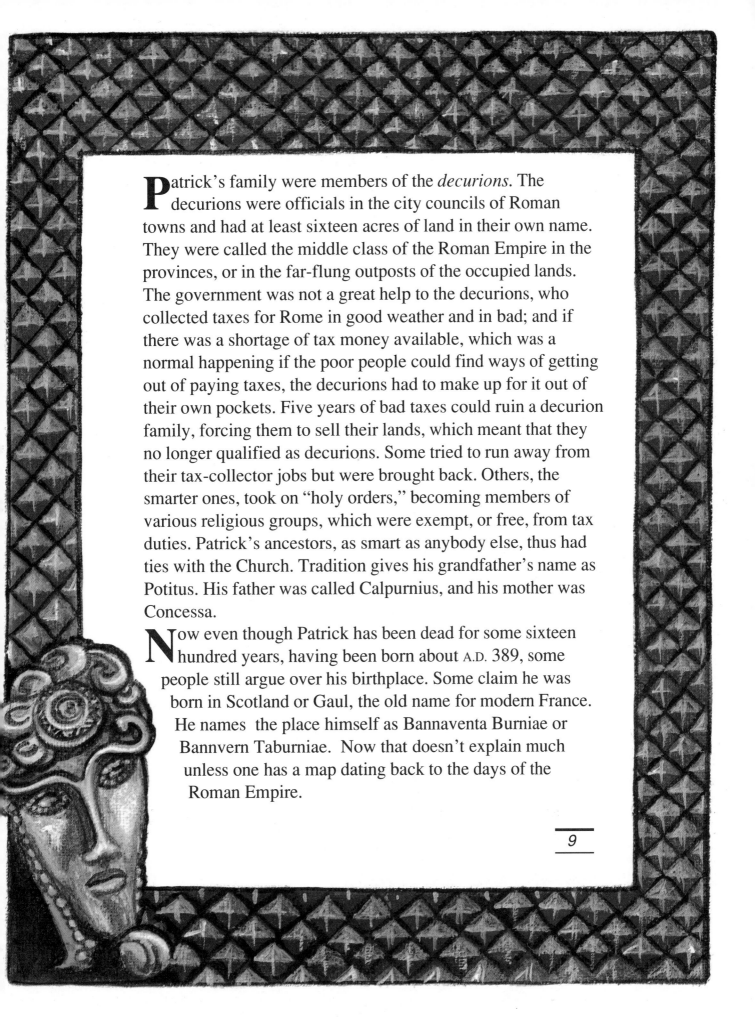

Patrick's family were members of the *decurions*. The decurions were officials in the city councils of Roman towns and had at least sixteen acres of land in their own name. They were called the middle class of the Roman Empire in the provinces, or in the far-flung outposts of the occupied lands. The government was not a great help to the decurions, who collected taxes for Rome in good weather and in bad; and if there was a shortage of tax money available, which was a normal happening if the poor people could find ways of getting out of paying taxes, the decurions had to make up for it out of their own pockets. Five years of bad taxes could ruin a decurion family, forcing them to sell their lands, which meant that they no longer qualified as decurions. Some tried to run away from their tax-collector jobs but were brought back. Others, the smarter ones, took on "holy orders," becoming members of various religious groups, which were exempt, or free, from tax duties. Patrick's ancestors, as smart as anybody else, thus had ties with the Church. Tradition gives his grandfather's name as Potitus. His father was called Calpurnius, and his mother was Concessa.

Now even though Patrick has been dead for some sixteen hundred years, having been born about A.D. 389, some people still argue over his birthplace. Some claim he was born in Scotland or Gaul, the old name for modern France. He names the place himself as Bannaventa Burniae or Bannvern Taburniae. Now that doesn't explain much unless one has a map dating back to the days of the Roman Empire.

9

Now even if one does have a map made in ancient Rome, the name of his hometown was really popular. There are Bannaventa Burniaes all over the place on the old maps. Recent studies, with and without arguments, however, show that Patrick lived in the western area of Britain, probably near the mouth of the River Bristol. Several historical facts point to that, and one of them consists of the records of Irish raids in the region. Secondly, there is an Irish tradition that Bannaventa Burniae isn't just a pretty name. It means "end of the River Severn," which would put Patrick and his birth near the Bay of Bristol.

It was a Roman settlement, run by a city council and using Roman laws. He was given the name Patricius Sucatus, but the name Patrick has done just fine over the centuries. Patrick was also well educated, both as a Christian and as a Roman, not that the two always worked for the same end in the world.

In some years the Christians were told they could worship freely and then a few months later they were thrown to the lions. Patrick, however, along with his family, was a true Roman, and together they looked to Rome as the source of law, culture, and protection in the wild lands of Britain. They did not understand that the Rome they loved was dying. Civil wars, political feuds, economic problems, and corruption were weakening the Empire and making it vulnerable to

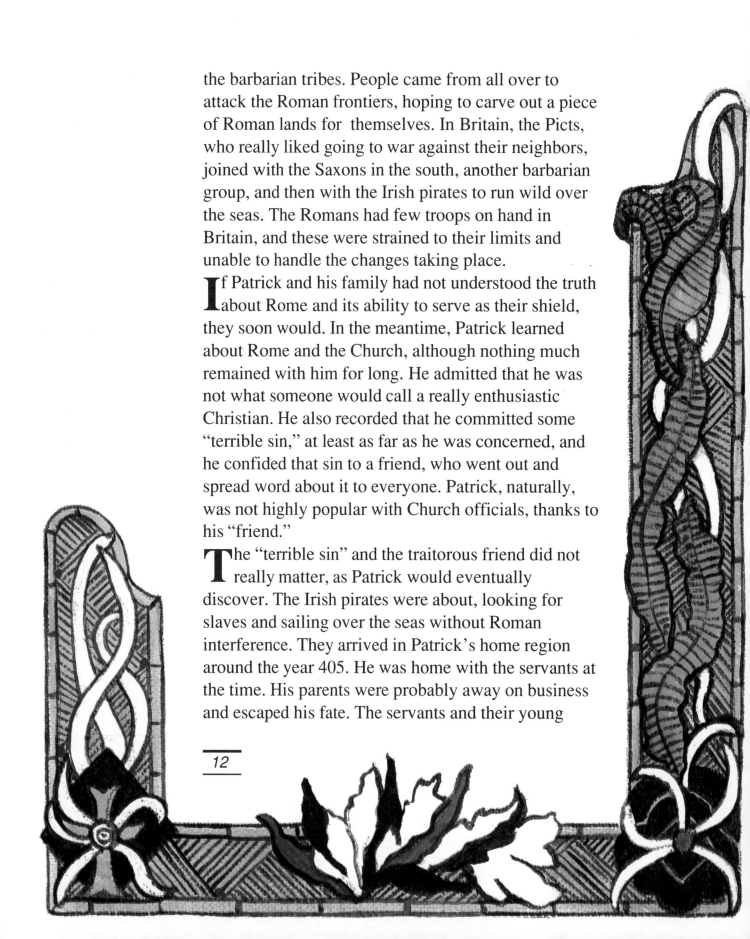

the barbarian tribes. People came from all over to attack the Roman frontiers, hoping to carve out a piece of Roman lands for themselves. In Britain, the Picts, who really liked going to war against their neighbors, joined with the Saxons in the south, another barbarian group, and then with the Irish pirates to run wild over the seas. The Romans had few troops on hand in Britain, and these were strained to their limits and unable to handle the changes taking place.

If Patrick and his family had not understood the truth about Rome and its ability to serve as their shield, they soon would. In the meantime, Patrick learned about Rome and the Church, although nothing much remained with him for long. He admitted that he was not what someone would call a really enthusiastic Christian. He also recorded that he committed some "terrible sin," at least as far as he was concerned, and he confided that sin to a friend, who went out and spread word about it to everyone. Patrick, naturally, was not highly popular with Church officials, thanks to his "friend."

The "terrible sin" and the traitorous friend did not really matter, as Patrick would eventually discover. The Irish pirates were about, looking for slaves and sailing over the seas without Roman interference. They arrived in Patrick's home region around the year 405. He was home with the servants at the time. His parents were probably away on business and escaped his fate. The servants and their young master were taken captive and dragged to the coast with ropes around their necks as the pirates laughed and hit them to keep up the pace. Patrick was put on board an Irish swift-sailing vessel called a *curach*. In his *Confession*, one of his books that have survived the centuries, he spoke about the pitiful state that he was in. Patrick was truly convinced that God was taking him and his countrymen and scattering them into all of the nations of the earth. In Patrick's case it was not exactly the far ends of the world, but it must have seemed that way to him. In order to make sure that he did not recognize any familiar landscape or find a way to escape, he was taken to Connaught (which nowadays is spelled "Connacht"). A man who farmed and ranched bought him and placed him in an area that Patrick described as "near the Wood of Voclut." This means he was in County Mayo, near Killala Bay, on the border of County Sligo. This is the northwestern part of Ireland.

Patrick was bought by the rancher so that he could work as a shepherd, which was quite a comedown for an educated Roman-Briton. The work meant that he had to live outdoors in the woods, in the fields, and even on the sides of mountains. He was also alone most of the time. His master did not mistreat him, but the harsh conditions made him miserable. Patrick faced winds, rain, biting frosts, and terrible cold. He had just been torn from his land, cast into a strange world, and he had no defenses at first against the natural weather patterns there.

People argue over the exact place that Patrick lived and worked. Irish communities throughout the land would like to claim him as one of their residents during that terrible period

of his life. He was no longer a human being but a slave, a piece of property that others could buy and sell, whip and starve. He also had no hope of escaping.

In that windswept wilderness, Patrick, alone and isolated, had time to think and remember his home, his loved ones, and the lessons that he had been taught as a child. He used the same method that many prisoners find helpful while in captivity. In order to keep himself from becoming a mindless idiot without hope or a single original thought, Patrick began a journey home deep within himself.

Each scene, each word, each lesson that he remembered linked him to his former life and told him that he was not an animal that could be herded over strange fields. Some prisoners find this method effective, while others sing songs, recite poetry, or quote passages from books they have read. In the process, Patrick was really surprised to find that the teachings about Christ and the Church came flooding into his mind. He said that he "turned with all my heart to the Lord my God who . . . guarded me before I knew him and had wisdom."

In other words, Patrick was growing up and realizing that he had been wrenched from his normal life in order to come to terms with things deep inside him.

Sitting on the side of the mountains, in the middle of nowhere, he began to accept Christ and His divine will. He knew that he would never be swayed from them again, as his heart and mind were being molded by his sorrows and his isolation. Shortly after this conversion took place, at the end of six years of slavery, Patrick heard a voice telling him that it was time for him to fast, to exercise, and to be ready to return to his native land. Later the voice announced: "Behold, thy ship is ready."

Patrick had to travel two hundred miles across Ireland in order to reach the sea, and it was not a friendly land to runaway slaves. He snatched food and drink where he could find it and hid from villagers and townspeople. His master was surely hunting for him, and if he was caught the punishment would be terrible. Reaching the coast, he saw a ship ready to sail, and he asked to come aboard as a passenger, one who would work for his passage. The captain of the ship was not agreeable, and it took Patrick some time and a lot of prayer before he was taken as a member of the crew. The ship was probably on its way to France, which was then called Gaul. It is believed that the ship was anchored at Inver-dea, at the mouth of the River Vitry, near Wicklow.

While sailing on the sea, Patrick was asked to sign a contract of service that would make him a permanent member of the ship's crew. He was not interested, but he cared about the men, who were pagans. When they landed eventually in Gaul — at least that is where most people think they landed — Patrick relates his adventures with the crew in the act of wandering for days in a "desert." Naturally, no one knows to this day just what he was talking about, as deserts are not part of the European landscape. Gaul, however, had been run over by barbarians, who took what they wanted and then put everything to the torch and burned everyone else to death. People such as the Vandals, ferocious and cruel hordes, raced across Europe at the time, leaving entire regions so destroyed that they would have looked like Patrick's "desert."

While wandering about in the "desert," the crew ran out of food, and the captain asked Patrick to prove his Christian faith by finding them something to keep them alive. Patrick replied: "Nothing is impossible for my God. Turn to Him sincerely and He may send food in your path this day until you are filled, for He has plenty in all places." No sooner were the words out of his mouth than a family of pigs, escaping the destruction, wandered past them. The crew killed, cooked, and ate the pigs; filled at last, the crew rested by the side of the road for two days.

Carrying the cargo from their ship on their backs, the crew avoided any horsemen on the road and stayed away from towns and villages, reaching their trading center inland in a matter of days. There, the captain, wanting his passage money and having no thought for Patrick's efforts on the road, sold him back into slavery.

16

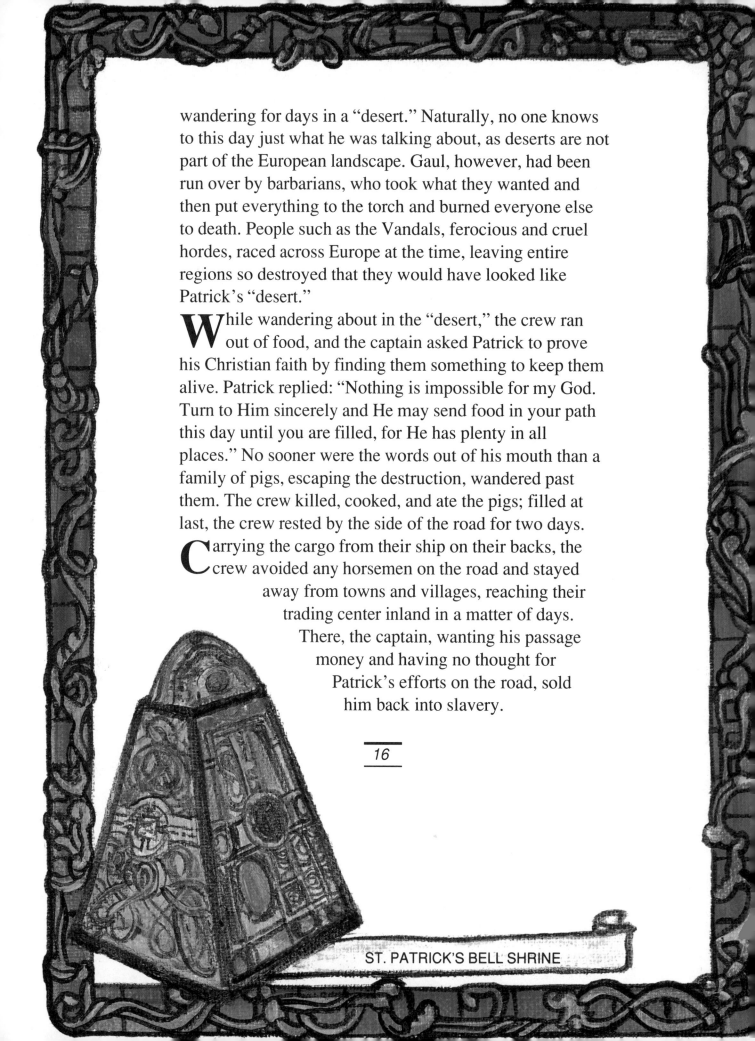

ST. PATRICK'S BELL SHRINE

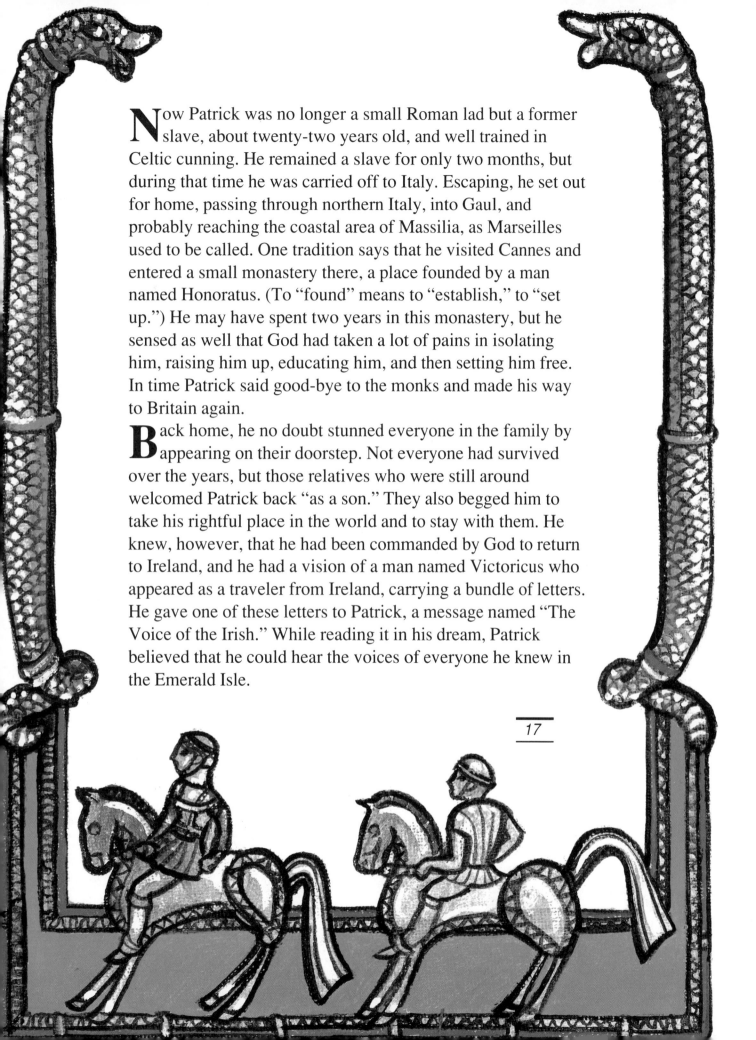

Now Patrick was no longer a small Roman lad but a former slave, about twenty-two years old, and well trained in Celtic cunning. He remained a slave for only two months, but during that time he was carried off to Italy. Escaping, he set out for home, passing through northern Italy, into Gaul, and probably reaching the coastal area of Massilia, as Marseilles used to be called. One tradition says that he visited Cannes and entered a small monastery there, a place founded by a man named Honoratus. (To "found" means to "establish," to "set up.") He may have spent two years in this monastery, but he sensed as well that God had taken a lot of pains in isolating him, raising him up, educating him, and then setting him free. In time Patrick said good-bye to the monks and made his way to Britain again.

Back home, he no doubt stunned everyone in the family by appearing on their doorstep. Not everyone had survived over the years, but those relatives who were still around welcomed Patrick back "as a son." They also begged him to take his rightful place in the world and to stay with them. He knew, however, that he had been commanded by God to return to Ireland, and he had a vision of a man named Victoricus who appeared as a traveler from Ireland, carrying a bundle of letters. He gave one of these letters to Patrick, a message named "The Voice of the Irish." While reading it in his dream, Patrick believed that he could hear the voices of everyone he knew in the Emerald Isle.

He could not continue to read the letter, knowing that this was a sign from God. The Irish have added the tradition that the voices that Patrick heard were of the young children of Fochlad, even those who were not yet born. Fochlad is the name used now for the Wood of Voclut, where Patrick and his sheep spent countless hours under the stars.

He was mature enough and wise enough in the ways of men and faith to know that he could not just catch a ship and sail to Ireland to begin preaching there. Only the full powers of grace, the faith, and the Church could arm him with the weapons that he needed to fight a deeply rooted pagan belief in Ireland. Tradition states that Patrick went to Auxerre to be ordained as a deacon, studying as well for the priesthood. After ordination, Patrick saw a petition that was sent to Pope Celestine I by the local clergy, asking that the Church send missionaries to the Emerald Isle.

Patrick was the obvious choice for such a post, but once again he was isolated and left alone. As mentioned earlier, he had confided his past to a "friend," who promptly ran all over town with accusations and a strange version of what he had heard. The elders of the community felt that they could not trust Patrick as a result. In time, of course, Patrick was cleared of all charges and rumors, having had a vision in which Almighty God had told him that anyone who tried to hurt him might just as well try to poke God in the eye.

A man named Palladius, chosen in the place of Patrick, went to Ireland and lasted just two years there, dying sometime around 432. Some people claim that Palladius was incompetent, a man who messed up things more than he helped them. Others believe that he did manage to start a few churches but then believed that he was called to convert the barbarian Picts in the north and started journeying to them. He died on the road to the Pict lands.

While Palladius was either doing well or badly, depending on the way one looks at him, Patrick was being consecrated a bishop of the Church. He was then given the post of missionary to Ireland, and he set about making preparations for his journey. Patrick knew that the Irish nobles and kings would not look with favor on a simple man, someone arriving without fine clothes, without treasures, money, religious articles, and the appearance of being prosperous. If a man looked wealthy, he obviously was a man of authority in the eyes of the chieftains of Erin. For this reason Patrick, as a bishop and as a man who understood the Celtic outlook on things, knew that he had to impress the Irish from the start. He no doubt had servants and fellow priests with him when he set sail, but there is no record as to their names or positions.

Now Patrick was not just another missionary going out to spread the light of Christ in the world. This was a slave returning to the sites of his sufferings. This was a former captive willing to die for the very people who had taken him away from all that he loved. Patrick went to Ireland because he knew that ignorance, stupidity, the lack of moral awareness, and the running after pleasures was the truest form of slavery. Men and women who want only the things of this world are chained to this world.

19

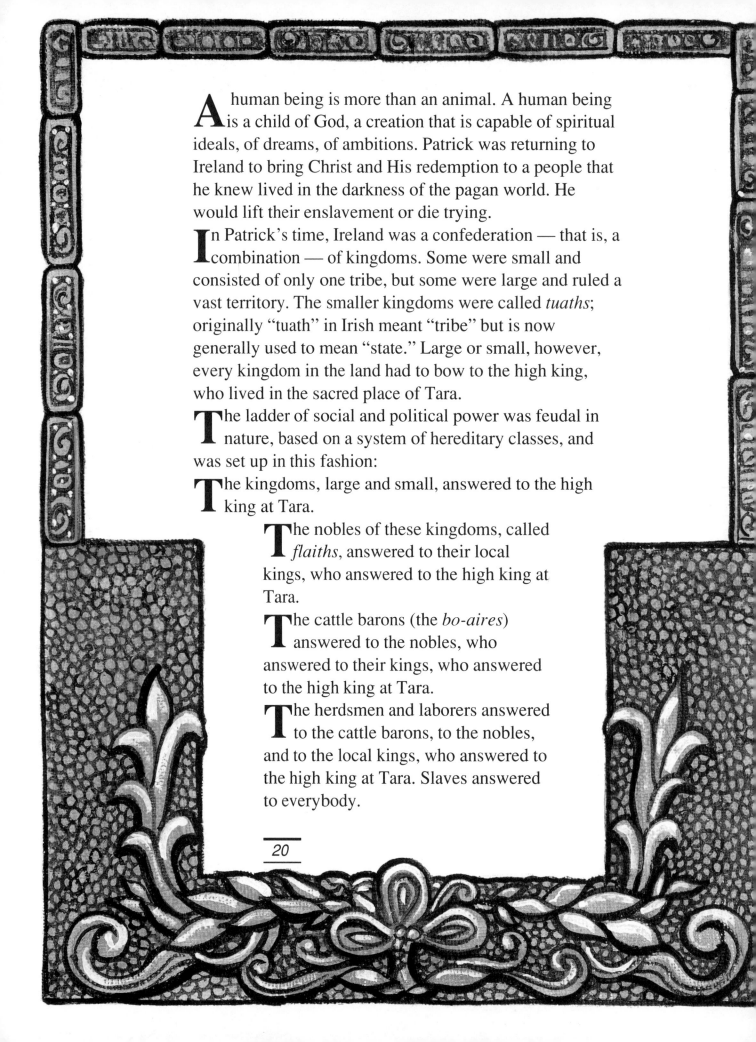

A human being is more than an animal. A human being is a child of God, a creation that is capable of spiritual ideals, of dreams, of ambitions. Patrick was returning to Ireland to bring Christ and His redemption to a people that he knew lived in the darkness of the pagan world. He would lift their enslavement or die trying.

In Patrick's time, Ireland was a confederation — that is, a combination — of kingdoms. Some were small and consisted of only one tribe, but some were large and ruled a vast territory. The smaller kingdoms were called *tuaths*; originally "tuath" in Irish meant "tribe" but is now generally used to mean "state." Large or small, however, every kingdom in the land had to bow to the high king, who lived in the sacred place of Tara.

The ladder of social and political power was feudal in nature, based on a system of hereditary classes, and was set up in this fashion:

The kingdoms, large and small, answered to the high king at Tara.

The nobles of these kingdoms, called *flaiths*, answered to their local kings, who answered to the high king at Tara.

The cattle barons (the *bo-aires*) answered to the nobles, who answered to their kings, who answered to the high king at Tara.

The herdsmen and laborers answered to the cattle barons, to the nobles, and to the local kings, who answered to the high king at Tara. Slaves answered to everybody.

20

As a slave, Patrick had been called a *fudir*, and he was at the bottom of the social and political heap in Ireland. The kings and nobles, naturally, held not only rank and hereditary titles but had the land as well. This means that this ruling class could control just about everybody by handing out bits and pieces of land in return for loyalty, that is, oaths of allegiance or services. If anyone wanted to rise in the ranks, that person had to be willing to work for it.

Patrick understood this system, and he knew that converting the slaves, the herders, the laborers, or even the cattle barons, would be useless. The cattle barons had wealth, but their assets were movable certainly. They owned no land. Without land, they had to answer to the nobles above them. The herders and laborers were not free either. They had to remain in one place, working for the pleasure of one individual or family. They did, however, belong to the local tribe. Converting these people would no doubt bring comfort to their souls, but it would not bring about the Christianization of Ireland. In many ways, starting at the bottom would cause the kings to oppose the Church. These kings would rightly believe that Christianity taught that each human being was equal in the sight of God, something that would certainly turn the Irish world upside down.

A TYPICAL IRISH KING

The problem was simple enough. Even the high kings of Ireland had political and social troubles. The kings of the various smaller realms ruled their own lands and settled their own tribal feuds, but they had to answer to the high king. They also envied his throne and were ready to take it over whenever they got the chance. The high kings actually ruled over Cashel, Connaught, Laigin, Aileach, Ulaid, and Oriel, with each region firmly in the hands of lesser kings who managed affairs there.

The high kings were not what were called absolute monarchs. Their word was not law on every occasion, and they had to work by consensus, that is, they had to find ways in which they convinced the lesser kings that the ideas they proposed were good and worth following. If the lesser kings or if the high king was impressed by Patrick and the Christian faith, the battle for the soul of Ireland was nearly won. Just converting a few families here and there was not the best policy. Actually, such families could be persecuted for the faith later on. Patrick could not begin with slaves, herdsmen, laborers, or even with the cattle barons. The nobles would dare to stand firm if they became Christians, but even they could be ruined or harmed by the kings. Patrick understood all of these aspects of Irish life as he sailed to the Emerald Isle. He had been prepared by Almighty God for his mission, and he would use every bit of information that he had to prepare the way for the faith.

Patrick also knew about the Celtic forms of paganism, all of which were deep-rooted and ancient. At one time, the famed Druids — those mysterious and intellectual priests of the old ways — worked in the British Isles. The Romans had recognized them as enemies and had slain most in Angelsey soon after they came to colonize Britain. What relationship the "Druids" of Ireland had to these British priests is not well known today. Actually, these Irish priests were perhaps not even Druids at all and should be called simply "pagan priests." Like the Druids, however, the Irish priests were learned men, that is to say, intelligent, well educated, and familiar with poetry, law, astronomy, and magic. The Irish pagan priests lacked one thing that had kept the Druids strong before the Romans killed them: a union and an organization. Because they were not well controlled or members of a national structure, the individual pagan priests were open to attack by Patrick.

Irish tradition says that the priests there had foretold that a strange new religion would come to the Emerald Isle, and that it would change forever the ways of the people, destroying the ancient pagan religion. The ceremonies that made up much of the pagan beliefs were normally held in wooded areas, and the sun was important to them, as the sun played a major role in most ancient cultures. If the sun fails, the earth dies, and it did not take primitive people very long to figure that out for themselves.

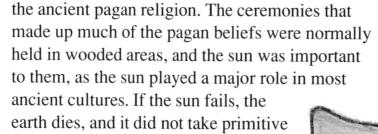

24

There were ancient gods and figures of legend in the Irish pagan beliefs, including fairies and "little people," still claimed to be seen by some in parts of Ireland today, especially after celebrations or festivals. The fairies, who were called the *sidhe*, were not called illusions by the early Christians in Ireland. Perhaps it was impossible to make people stop seeing them, or perhaps they were so much a part of the Irish landscape that no one could put them away without causing grief.

There was another aspect to Patrick's arrival as well, and that was the shadow of Rome over that part of the world — over most of the known world to be exact. The Irish were well acquainted with the Roman Empire, having seen its armies, its government, and its ability to transform entire regions. The Irish had also had dealings with the Romans over the decades, and they had heard of the Christian faith. This creed of the Romans, while not accepted by the Irish, had a unique prestige, a rank of honor, among them. Even as the Romans began to pull back from Britain, the Christian faith remained a faith of prestige in Irish eyes. Patrick was counting on that fact to aid him in his mission. He knew that the high king and others would receive him with courtesy because he represented Rome and the Church.

The various members of the Church in Britain, naturally, had their own ideas about what Patrick was expected to accomplish in Ireland. Many felt that his main work was to serve and support the few Christian converts already in the Emerald Isle. They did not think about a program to convert the entire population. Patrick did! His main efforts were to convert the high king, the lesser kings, and every other class of society. The fact that this ambition would work him almost to death, and the fact that his life would be in danger, did not make him hesitate. Patrick was going back to the land of his slavery, and he was going to win the Irish people to the Cross of Christ.

He probably entered Ireland at the coastal inlet at Vartry, which was north of Wicklow. This was the usual first point of contact for ships coming from Britain or the European continent. The advantages of the Vartry port were the fact that it was an easy place to land, and it opened the way for political sites of importance. Palladius had come this way before Patrick, and when word reached the converts in the area, they came to welcome their new bishop to the land.

There are many traditions about Patrick's first days in Ireland. One places him in northern Ireland, in the village of Ulida, specifically in the area of D'un Lethglasse. There he supposedly went for a walk with his aides and was seen by a swineherd, who ran to tell his master. The master was one Dichu, reported as a man of infinite goodness. Originally planning to kill Patrick and the other strangers, a custom of defense in those times, instead he invited the group into his home. Patrick, preaching to the man, made his first convert in Ireland. The man named Dichu really did live, and he was a local nobleman who gave Patrick a small piece of land and a wooden barn that was converted into a site of Christian worship.

Whether Patrick visited Dichu first or made his way directly, he set out for Tara, the seat of the high king. Many traditions speak of his arrival there, the most interesting being his lighting of the paschal fire, the fire burned at the Easter celebrations.

27

Patrick decided to celebrate Easter soon after arriving in the area, and he intended to light a fire on the high hill of Slane, which overlooks the River Boyne, about twelve miles from the residence of the high king at Tara, in Meath. It was a custom in the land that no fire could be lit until the royal fire was ignited and blazing into the night on the eve of Easter. Anyone daring to violate this tradition faced bad luck and probably the anger of the king.

The high king at the time was a man named Loigaire, the son of King Niall, who had died in battle while on a raid in Britain. Loigaire had succeeded to the throne in 428 or thereabouts and was generally recorded as being wise and fair. He recognized the fact that Christianity had entered Ireland and also understood the dangers that the new religion posed for Erin's past traditions and knowledge. The pagans were on one side, and the Christians were on the other. His own son, Fedilmid, had become a Christian probably through contact with the British Romans, and perhaps even through the efforts of Palladius and others. The king's grandson, Fortchernn, was a Christian also.

This was probably why Loigaire and his court sat in darkness on Easter eve, waiting for the official lighting of the flame. Looking out the window, however, the entire court saw a flame burning on the hill of Slane. His councilors, the men who were chosen to advise him, told Loigaire that if he did not put that flame out it would burn down the entire land. He had no choice but to mount up and go kill the man who had started the fire.

The high king was warned by his sorcerers — his magicians — not to go near the fire because that would identify him as a worshiper. Because of this warning, Loigaire therefore sent for Patrick to appear before him. The sorcerers then told everyone to stay seated when Patrick arrived, because rising out of respect would again mark them as worshipers. Sorcerers and court councilors worried about things like that all of the time. As Patrick approached, however, a man named Erc rose up to salute him and was blessed in return. When Erc died — probably of old age, by the way — he was honored by being buried on Slane.

Tradition states that the sorcerers tried spells, insults, shouts, arguments, perhaps even a certain mild violence, in order to make Patrick flee. He did not. He stayed and listened to one and all, until Loigaire returned to Tara, confused and annoyed by the entire evening. No one knows if this tradition is accurate or not, but it is known that Patrick did arrive at Tara in order to deal with the high king. That was his entire purpose, after all, the reason for his being in Ireland.

When he was received at court, Loigaire knew well the fact that Patrick represented Rome and the Church. He was also aware of the fact that many Irish were becoming Christians. Because of these two realities, he agreed to give Patrick his royal protection and to be tolerant about the faith in the region. Loigaire, however, had no intention of being baptized, and even if he had he could not have won over all of Ireland with that action.

Having gained royal protection, Patrick set out to establish churches in Ireland and to make Christianity a permanent presence among the people. An early triumph was the conversion of Conall, the son of King Niall and the brother of King Loigaire. Conall was baptized by Patrick and granted the Church a piece of land for the building of a large place of worship.

Such conversions and even the royal approval brought Patrick many enemies, of course. There were many in Ireland who wanted all trace of Christianity erased. Patrick received death threats from those Irish lords who believed that the faith would bring an end to their power. Others, having been raised in the pagan rites of ancient Ireland, wanted no part of the new Church and were quite willing to see Patrick dead if that would bring Christianity to a halt. Patrick understood their feelings and their hatred. He also knew that each time he went into a different part of Ireland he was risking his mission and his life. That did not stop him. The ex-slave walked across the green hills and the lovely dales, bringing the Cross of Christ to everyone that he met. If they cursed him or threw stones, it did not matter. If the Irish threatened his life, that was only temporary. In time, he knew, they would accept the faith and allow it to shine with a beautiful luster, a pure light, in Erin.

After working in Meath, Patrick went to the kingdom of Connaught, or at least that is what the legends say. The object of his attention there was a huge idol that stood in the area, known as Cenn Cruaich or Crom Cruaich, the depiction of Mag Slecht, an ancient god of the region. Patrick wanted to show the power of the Church, and he knew that by striking at the idol, which was a golden statue, he could strike terror into the hearts of the people. The pagans put a lot of faith in their idols. If someone just walked up and knocked one over without being struck dead by the god, the power of the old ways was shattered as easily as the stone. He smashed the Cenn Cruaich with his crosier — that is, his bishop's staff — and the people waited, saw nothing happened, and then wailed as they realized that the ancient ways were done.

This is probably a tale that grew out of Patrick's labors in Ireland. The chroniclers of the time did not mention Mag Slecht being knocked over, and certainly one of them would have noted such a dramatic event. Like other legends about Patrick, this one was started to display Patrick's power to confront the chains of darkness and superstition that had held Ireland and other lands for so many centuries. Many pagan religions of the time were based on blood and sacrifice, and they kept the people terrorized and ignorant.

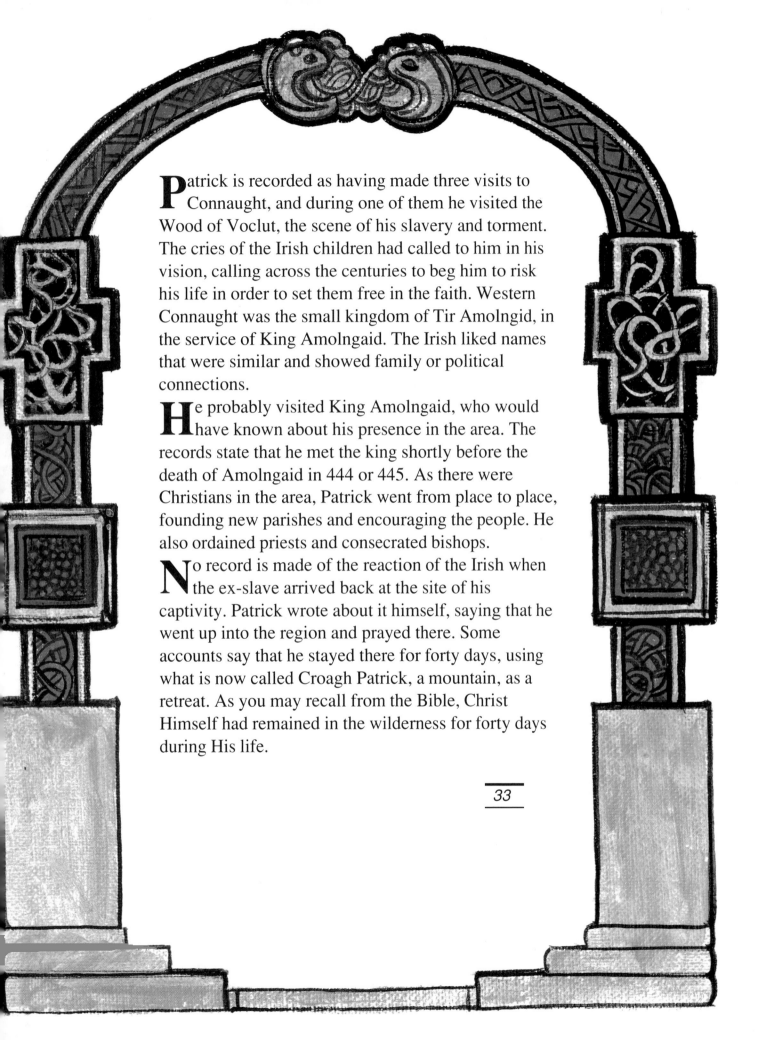

Patrick is recorded as having made three visits to Connaught, and during one of them he visited the Wood of Voclut, the scene of his slavery and torment. The cries of the Irish children had called to him in his vision, calling across the centuries to beg him to risk his life in order to set them free in the faith. Western Connaught was the small kingdom of Tir Amolngid, in the service of King Amolngaid. The Irish liked names that were similar and showed family or political connections.

He probably visited King Amolngaid, who would have known about his presence in the area. The records state that he met the king shortly before the death of Amolngaid in 444 or 445. As there were Christians in the area, Patrick went from place to place, founding new parishes and encouraging the people. He also ordained priests and consecrated bishops.

No record is made of the reaction of the Irish when the ex-slave arrived back at the site of his captivity. Patrick wrote about it himself, saying that he went up into the region and prayed there. Some accounts say that he stayed there for forty days, using what is now called Croagh Patrick, a mountain, as a retreat. As you may recall from the Bible, Christ Himself had remained in the wilderness for forty days during His life.

33

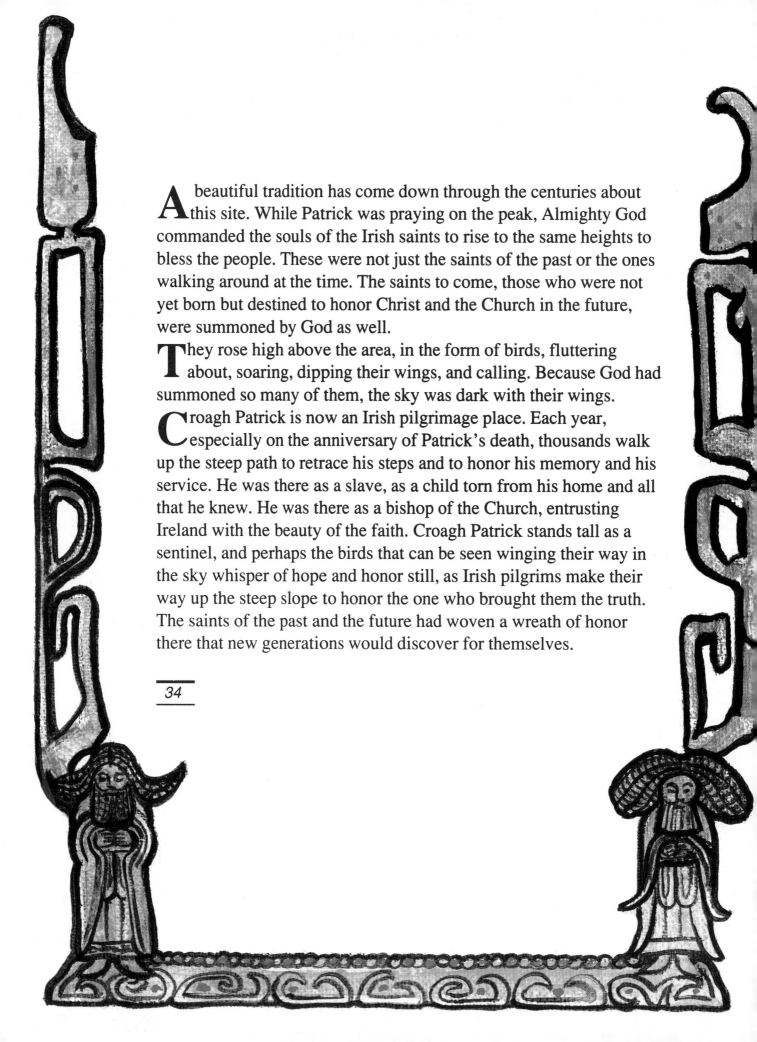

A beautiful tradition has come down through the centuries about this site. While Patrick was praying on the peak, Almighty God commanded the souls of the Irish saints to rise to the same heights to bless the people. These were not just the saints of the past or the ones walking around at the time. The saints to come, those who were not yet born but destined to honor Christ and the Church in the future, were summoned by God as well.

They rose high above the area, in the form of birds, fluttering about, soaring, dipping their wings, and calling. Because God had summoned so many of them, the sky was dark with their wings.

Croagh Patrick is now an Irish pilgrimage place. Each year, especially on the anniversary of Patrick's death, thousands walk up the steep path to retrace his steps and to honor his memory and his service. He was there as a slave, as a child torn from his home and all that he knew. He was there as a bishop of the Church, entrusting Ireland with the beauty of the faith. Croagh Patrick stands tall as a sentinel, and perhaps the birds that can be seen winging their way in the sky whisper of hope and honor still, as Irish pilgrims make their way up the steep slope to honor the one who brought them the truth. The saints of the past and the future had woven a wreath of honor there that new generations would discover for themselves.

34

Converting an entire nation to the faith takes more than visits and sermons. Patrick, aware of the political and religious traditions of Ireland, set out for Rome — probably between 441 and 443 — in order to explain his work and the Irish to the Holy Father, Pope Leo the Great. It was important that the Pope hear the story of Ireland face to face. Leo was the one who could give Patrick the sort of support that he needed to complete his work. The Church there could provide him with religious objects and the necessary vestments and altar pieces for the growing parishes.

Patrick also knew that he had to found a central seat of power for the faith, a place that would be called a metropolitan church. Such a center would organize the faithful and keep the Church secure. His talks with Pope Leo the Great must have been exciting for both of them. These were men dedicated to bringing Christ to every nation in the world. Patrick also loved Ireland, its beauty, its rich traditions, its arts, and the warm and willing hearts of the Irish people. When he finished with his visit, he had everything that he needed. An official record states that "he was approved in the Catholic faith."

35

Upon his return to Ireland, sometime in 444, Patrick started building his metropolitan church at Armagh. He chose Armagh because of its location, where the church could be positioned on a high hill. Ardd Mache, translated as "the Height of Macha," was supposedly named after a great heroine of Irish legend. The land was under the control of King Daire, probably the ruler of Oriel, a man quite tolerant of the local Christians. Because of Daire's reputation for fairness, the Christians begged him for a grant of land, and they received a parcel at the base of Ardd Mache. The first piece of land was a large circular space, enclosed by an earthen rampart, a wall. Within this wall was a home for monks. Patrick, seeing the area, wanted the high hill for the church and asked Daire for it. He received a smaller hill instead, that is until two things happened to change Daire's mind.

Soon after Patrick obtained the land grant, a royal squire rode to the monastery and insisted that he be allowed to graze his horse in a field during the night. Patrick agreed, and the next morning the squire came to the field and found the horse dead. The squire, naturally, claimed that Patrick and his people had killed the horse out of spite.

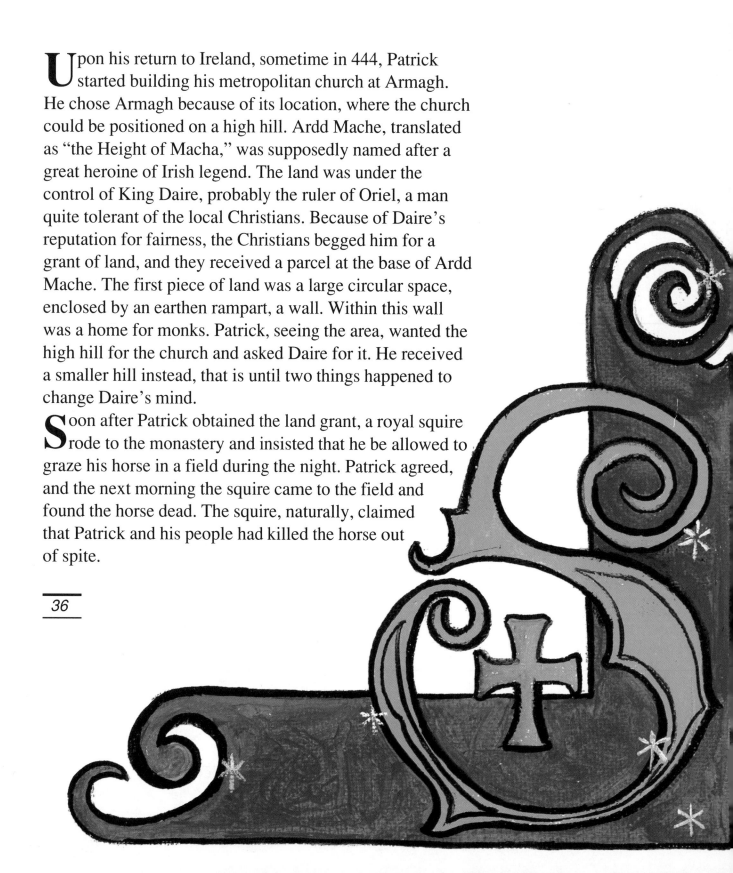

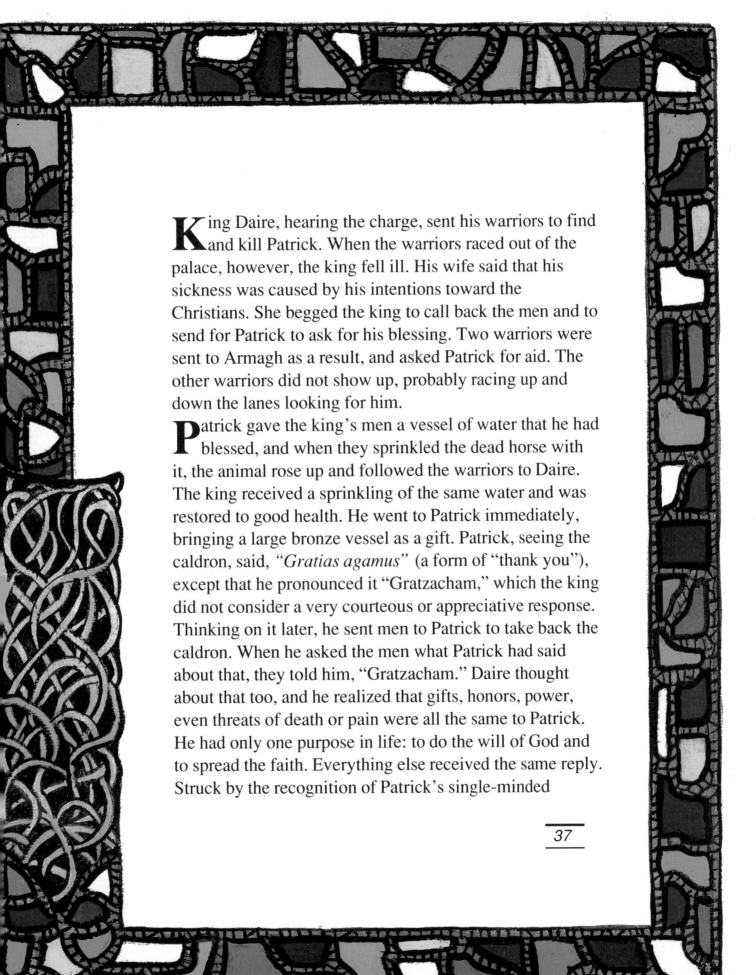

King Daire, hearing the charge, sent his warriors to find and kill Patrick. When the warriors raced out of the palace, however, the king fell ill. His wife said that his sickness was caused by his intentions toward the Christians. She begged the king to call back the men and to send for Patrick to ask for his blessing. Two warriors were sent to Armagh as a result, and asked Patrick for aid. The other warriors did not show up, probably racing up and down the lanes looking for him.

Patrick gave the king's men a vessel of water that he had blessed, and when they sprinkled the dead horse with it, the animal rose up and followed the warriors to Daire. The king received a sprinkling of the same water and was restored to good health. He went to Patrick immediately, bringing a large bronze vessel as a gift. Patrick, seeing the caldron, said, *"Gratias agamus"* (a form of "thank you"), except that he pronounced it "Gratzacham," which the king did not consider a very courteous or appreciative response. Thinking on it later, he sent men to Patrick to take back the caldron. When he asked the men what Patrick had said about that, they told him, "Gratzacham." Daire thought about that too, and he realized that gifts, honors, power, even threats of death or pain were all the same to Patrick. He had only one purpose in life: to do the will of God and to spread the faith. Everything else received the same reply. Struck by the recognition of Patrick's single-minded

37

approach to his mission, Daire gave him the hill on which the metropolitan church of Ireland would be raised up for Christ and His own.

Now, just building a lot of fancy parishes and monasteries does not make the faith strong in any country. Patrick wanted to change the way the Irish thought about life itself, and for this he needed a good many priests. Monks and nuns came, and they brought the prayers and sacrifices of the religious life to Ireland, a side of the Church that remains hidden but one that brings the graces for those who work in the missions and among the faithful. The women who came to the convents were called the "virgins of Christ," and many of these nuns faced family arguments over their joining the convent. They went anyway into the religious life, starting the great Irish tradition of service to the Church and to the Lord.

Patrick was also anxious to draw young Irish men into the priesthood, knowing that each nation needs its own young people in the lead. These priests, drawn from all walks of life, aware of the traditions and the customs of the Irish people, were able to talk to their own, instructing them in the faith. Patrick also consecrated the bishop of Armagh, choosing Benignus, a man who had become one of his followers from the beginning of the mission.

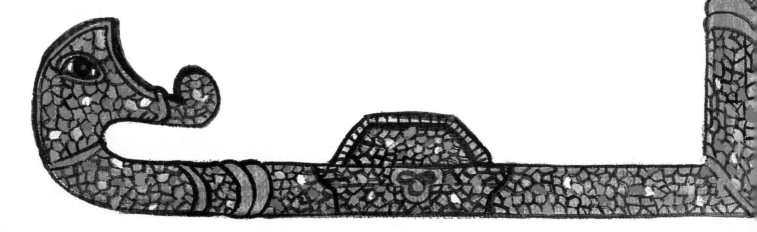

Laws and regulations were drawn up, and the Irish Church entered into the family of Christian people everywhere in the world. The monasteries were devoted to the same prayers and services as their counterparts across Europe so that the praise and the beautiful hymns that echoed in Rome in the dawning hours of the morning could be heard chiming across the beautiful land of Eire. If priests came from other lands to preach, they had to have written letters of permission from Armagh. Patrick did not intend to allow just anybody to speak to the Irish.

He was right about the Irish all along. He had started with the nobles, knowing that they would influence their own tenant farmers and peasants. Gifts were a weapon of the faith with such aristocrats. The Irish believed that gifts were tokens of good will, at least in the beginning. At the same time, gifts could keep nobles happy enough not to plunder, rob, or cheat the new parishes. Patrick dealt with such nobles in a patient, tolerant, and truthful way. When his converts did not always live up to their new faith, he did not shout at them or give them terrible penances. He understood that the faith was something new and precious for a people long held by the chains of superstition and darkness. Being severe would only have driven them away. Patrick won their hearts and their minds with laughter, with kindness, and with love.

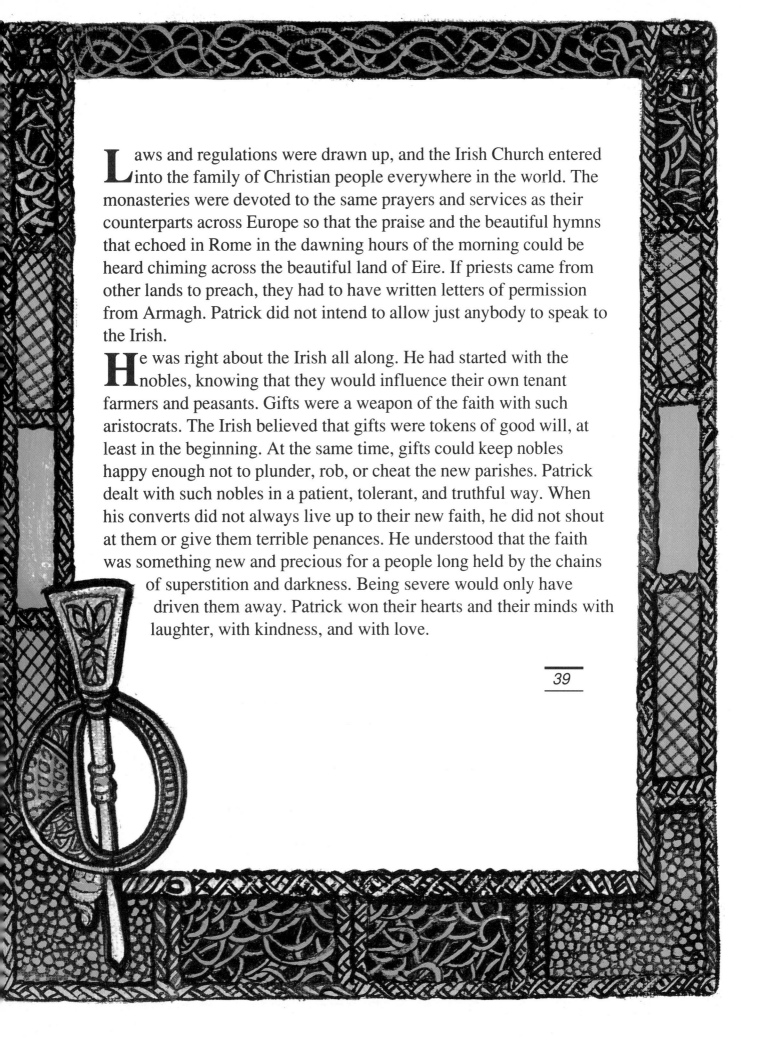

39

Behind the great missionary, behind the bishop's title and crosier (that is, his ceremonial staff), behind the vestments and the gifts, Patrick had come home again. It is sometimes easy to lose sight of a human being living a daily life, suffering, hoping, knowing fear and anxiety. No man or woman arrives in a mission field ready to die and completely prepared as to the best way in which to make friends for the Church. Patrick came better prepared than most because he had his old Roman training for organization and a deep love for the people who had enslaved him.

All of the legends about Patrick speak of his miracles, his courage, his honor. Underneath these outward signs, however, a human being walked alone among strangers, among enemies, even among those who wished him dead. The hills of Ireland and the beautiful streams and lakes restored him. The wind rustling through the trees or racing across the meadows called to him, and the terrible, stark grandeur of the land filled him with resolve. Patrick took all of these natural wonders and fed his courage with them.

The Irish people themselves, with their beautiful smiles and their gentle humor, restored Patrick as he lived among them. Always willing to laugh, even as nature crushed their farmlands or filled their fields with frost and destructive winds, the Irish must have given Patrick the warmth that he needed to endure. Patrick loved the Irish people and they, in turn, loved him, as the past several centuries have shown.

40

Not much has been written about the men who walked with Patrick either, but we know that they were brave, humble, and decent individuals who faced the same threats and terrors as their leader. Patrick was ever on the move, spending a good deal of time in northern Ireland, for example, and he would not have made the journeys alone. Kingdoms such as Munster and Leinster, for instance, had to be carefully won over. Traditions state that Patrick performed all sorts of miracles in these regions, which is a good way of attracting attention.

One of the most famous stories of Patrick's work in Munster concerns the famous Rock of Cashel, a huge tower of earth that rises out of the plain in the modern county of Tipperary. The region was ruled by King Oengus, from his castle on Cashel. This king woke up one morning and found that the statues of the old gods had tumbled from their places during the night and were smashed. Patrick arrived soon after, and the king, an intelligent man, welcomed him warmly. He probably thought the Rock of Cashel would come crashing down around his ears if he didn't extend every courtesy. Oengus even agreed to baptism, and Patrick performed the ceremony. During the service, however, Patrick accidentally ran the tip of his crosier through Oengus's foot. As the king did not cry out or hit him, Patrick did not know what he had just done until he looked down and saw the results of the terrible accident. He begged the king's pardon and asked Oengus why he had not protested or complained. The king

THE ROCK OF CASHEL

stated simply, in a true Irish warrior way, that he thought the stabbing of his foot was part of the Christian ceremony. Patrick stayed a long time in Munster — some accounts say seven years. How could one abandon a king like Oengus?

In time, however, the Apostle of Ireland — as Patrick is sometimes called — moved to Tipperary, where another legendary event took place. While on his way through the region, Patrick stopped to wash at a ford, a shallow area of the river, to wash his hands. One of his teeth, probably aged and rotted, fell out of his mouth and splashed into the water. Anxious to find it, Patrick groped around a bit and then climbed a nearby hill to see if he could discover some sign of the tooth in the water. He even had his companions look for it, knowing it would glisten in the water. When the tooth was recovered, the ford was ever after remembered as the scene of this personal part of Patrick's life, being called Ath Fiacla, the "Ford of the Tooth." The church built beside the stream was known as the Cell Fiacla, the "Church of the Tooth." Patrick, it seems, gave the tooth to four of his companions, telling them to build on the spot. Even today the area echoes with this tradition. It is called Kilfeakle, still in the county of Tipperary. The entire nation, in fact, resounds with echoes of Patrick's life and times, with amusing bits of legend and tradition about his ways and his goals.

These legends are the Irish way of keeping Patrick alive, and they are invaluable because so few actual historical records of his work remain. As Patrick was growing old in the missionary work, he started to deal with a man called Coroticus, and he supposedly wrote him a letter, called, naturally, the "Letter to Coroticus." Coroticus was a Christian chieftain who governed a small region in modern Scotland, known today as Strathclyde. This chief ruled from Ail Cluade, or "the Rock of Clyde." Coroticus was known as a warrior who sacked his neighbors often. He did this in order to raise money for his troops and government. The Irish and others sacked often, which is an old term meaning to attack, rob, steal, loot, and then destroy a region. Sometimes the warriors just attacked, robbed, stole, and looted, leaving the people a little something to get started again so they could come back another time and find them prosperous enough to sack all over. One of Coroticus's groups set out and reached the coast at Dalaradia. Moving inland, they were joined by a band of Picts, people who teamed up with anyone bent on sacking.

Their first victims were Christians, who were newly baptized and still dressed in white. Many were slain — that is, killed — and others were carried away. These would end up as Scottish slaves, as Patrick knew too well from personal experience.

44

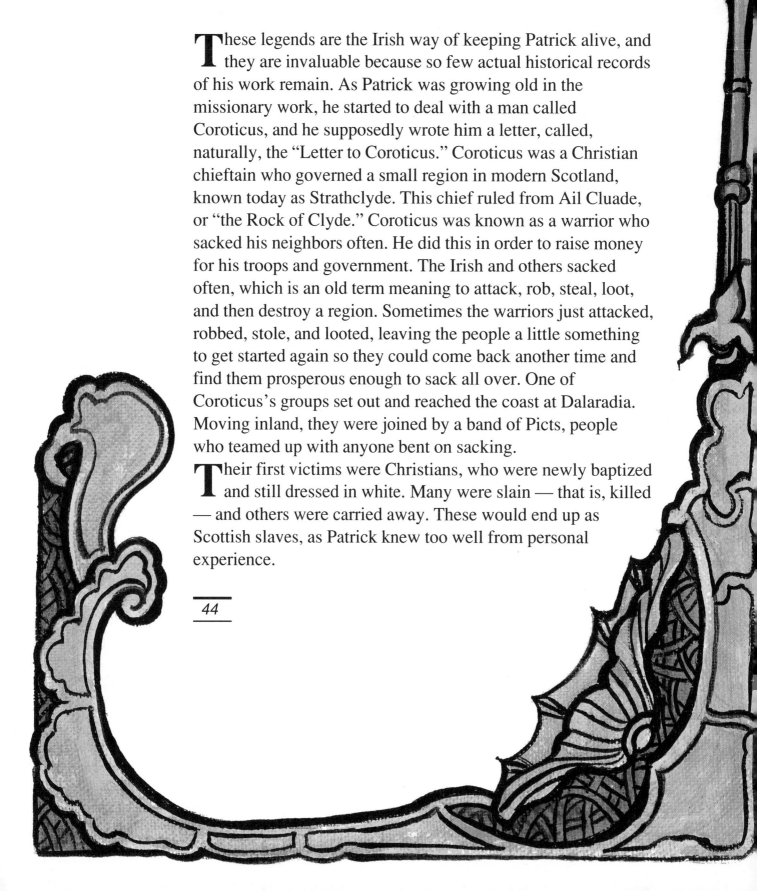

A CELTIC CRUCIFIX

A priest was sent immediately to the Picts and the Scots to ask for the release of the captives, but the warriors laughed at him. Coroticus was not among the group apparently. In Patrick's eyes, however, this Christian king might as well have struck the first blow, because he was responsible. Patrick took the battle to the Scottish Christians instead, calling on them to avoid contact with the "tyrant" and to refuse to even eat or drink with the soldiers of Coroticus until the captives were returned. No historical record gives any information about the outcome, but Coroticus and others were feeling the weight of Patrick's presence in the region.

Naturally, the letter and other events made Patrick's rivals and enemies even more angry. They accused him of being ambitious and so ignorant of literature and the arts that he was unfit to lead the Irish Church. As a result, Patrick was urged by his companions to put down his own thoughts, and he did so in a document called his *Confession*. This is an important work because it gives the modern world a genuine look at the real Patrick as he lived and breathed and worked in the world. He starts the work by calling himself "a sinner, a most simple countryman, the least of all the faithful and most contemptible to many. . . ."

Human beings have a way of attacking anyone who tries to do good. People become uneasy when they find out that an individual is making an effort to accomplish something fine. Perhaps it is because such a person makes everyone else look bad, or maybe people feel guilty about just going their own way without trying to do anything themselves about the world's

problems. It is easier to do nothing and then poke fun at the few who try to ease the pains and the suffering around them.

Patrick's main enemies were in Britain, naturally, because he had come from there originally and had managed his mission without begging for help or advice. Patrick admits freely that his Latin was bad. He also states that everything that he tried and accomplished was commanded by God. His humility, his continual reference to himself as a nobody, played into the hands of his enemies at the time. They read his work, declared him a numbskull, and laughed away his conversion of Ireland.

That outlook did not last long. The very people who made fun of Patrick died unknown and forgotten. Patrick remained. The writers coming behind him picked up the threads of his life and wove a splendid tapestry of courage and faith that has inspired generations over the centuries. Patrick would have said, "Gratzacham."

Like other saints before and after him, he knew that he had to leave his reputation and the success of his work in the hands of God. There are enough things happening to each human being without taking on worries about the future as well. Patrick lived each day as it came to him from God, and he worked until he dropped from exhaustion.

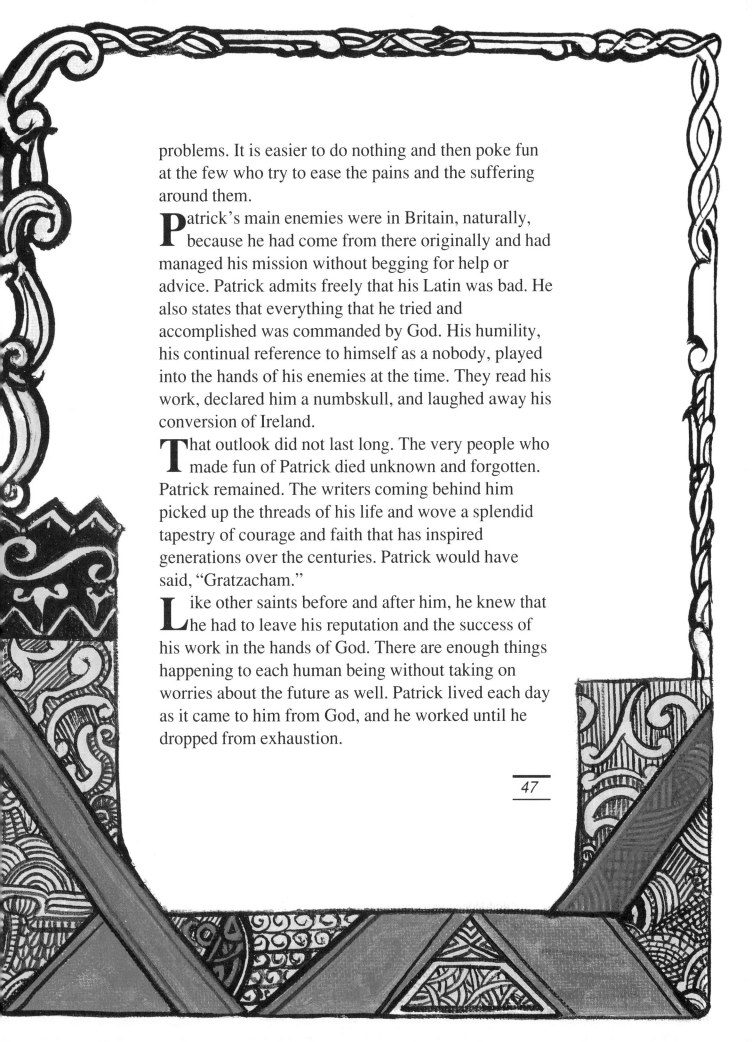

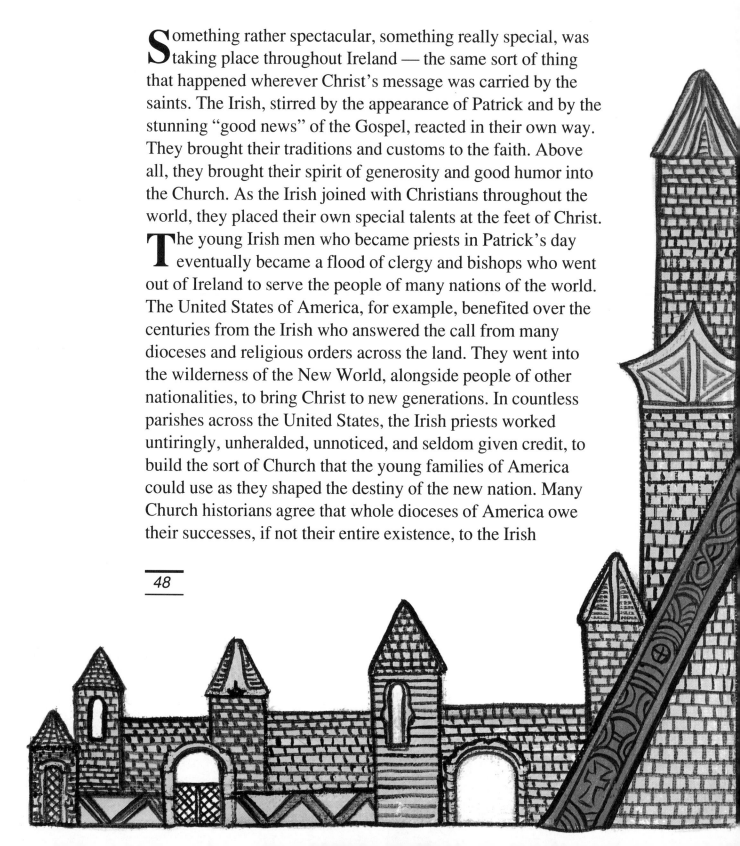

Something rather spectacular, something really special, was taking place throughout Ireland — the same sort of thing that happened wherever Christ's message was carried by the saints. The Irish, stirred by the appearance of Patrick and by the stunning "good news" of the Gospel, reacted in their own way. They brought their traditions and customs to the faith. Above all, they brought their spirit of generosity and good humor into the Church. As the Irish joined with Christians throughout the world, they placed their own special talents at the feet of Christ.

The young Irish men who became priests in Patrick's day eventually became a flood of clergy and bishops who went out of Ireland to serve the people of many nations of the world. The United States of America, for example, benefited over the centuries from the Irish who answered the call from many dioceses and religious orders across the land. They went into the wilderness of the New World, alongside people of other nationalities, to bring Christ to new generations. In countless parishes across the United States, the Irish priests worked untiringly, unheralded, unnoticed, and seldom given credit, to build the sort of Church that the young families of America could use as they shaped the destiny of the new nation. Many Church historians agree that whole dioceses of America owe their successes, if not their entire existence, to the Irish

priests who came to work among the people. Many of these priests, in turn, became prelates, or members of the ranks of the bishops and archbishops of the world. The Irish clergy led the way in generosity, service, devotion, and care.

Above all, these priests brought a love of Mary, a devotion to the Blessed Trinity, and a sense of honor in their calling. This was part of Patrick's legacy to the world. This is perhaps one of the reasons that St. Patrick's Day is a celebration in many lands.

It must be remembered that the Irish suffered a great deal in America when they first arrived. Many were treated harshly, kept out of certain areas, and discriminated against in others. The Irish, however, were hardier than other people, and they laughed, kept the faith alive, and continued to chase their dreams. At their side were the Irish priests, who came to serve their spiritual needs, to build churches, and to remember Patrick. These sons and daughters of Patrick — the lads he raised up to serve at the altars, the women who entered convents and taught the young or cared for the sick and poor, the families who struggled against all odds to raise their own and to keep the faith alive — are all part of Patrick's gift to the modern generation.

49

ST. PATRICK

In the legends about Patrick, his most charming feat, or act, concerns his chasing the snakes out of the island. Statues and paintings of Patrick show him frequently with a reptile at his feet, forcing it into the earth. These portraits are taken as proof that Patrick did chase all the serpents from Erin. Actually, there never were any snakes reported in Ireland. Patrick would have had a hard time chasing away creatures that were never there.

This doesn't mean that Patrick did not clear Ireland of serpents. The ancient religions of the world used the snake, the dragon (a make-believe flying reptile), and other reptiles as symbols of the powers of the gods. Patrick rid Ireland of the ancient superstitions, freed the children of future generations from the darkness of pagan traditions and sacrifices. In this way he certainly did rid Ireland of serpents.

The earliest writers about Patrick did not speak of his clearing the land of serpents. They did not understand, perhaps, that snakes take on a special symbolism of their own in legends and in tales told around fireplaces and hearths. Patrick freed Ireland of the serpent's hold, and he is honored as doing that by traditions. It is a nice way of saying that he cleaned out the nests of sin on the island.

51

Another tradition that has come down through the centuries is the association of Patrick with the shamrock. Shamrocks were always popular in Ireland. The three-leaved symbol can be seen throughout the world in various forms, connected in many lands to the clover variety of plants. Patrick did use the shamrock because the three leaves demonstrated the truth of the Most Blessed Trinity to a country people. Each leaf stood for the Father, the Son, and the Holy Spirit, as one, as a living insignia of the truths of the faith.

The origin of the shamrock's importance in Ireland dates back to truly ancient times. People always liked the shamrock, and, by the seventeenth century, coins and other objects carried the image of the plant. In Kilkenny, for example, the coins carried symbols of Patrick holding a shamrock. The shamrock had other purposes, of course; for instance, chewing a shamrock sweetens one's breath. The Irish often ate shamrocks with watercress, and shamrocks became part of the Irish diet in some parts of the country. By the eighteenth century, in fact, people not only ate shamrocks but wore them in their hats as a symbol of the faith and as a memorial to Patrick, the ex-slave.

For the modern world, of course, the shamrock has become an Irish image, brought out each March when the cities and towns of the earth celebrate St. Patrick's Day, March seventeenth. As green as the hills of Erin, and still forming the sign of the Most Blessed Trinity for all to see, the shamrock is Patrick's gift to the people of every age.

52

As the years passed in Ireland, as the seasons came to kiss Ireland's beautiful hills and dales, or to blanket them with frost and icy winds, Patrick continued his work. He grew old among the Irish, seeing the faith blossom and a new generation of young men and women rise up to bring the Christian message to the Emerald Isle. Throughout his long years of laboring among the Irish, Patrick is reported to have been visited by an angel named Victor. Victor was the one destined to tell Patrick of his coming death.

Patrick, aware of the fact that his strength was leaving him, was preparing to go to his beloved Armagh. Victor came to him, however, with the news that Armagh was not the place where his bones would rest for all time. He was to return to County Down, where God had willed that his grave would bless the land forever. In Down he would wait for the final resurrection, as his lifework would endure. The angel even described the manner in which Patrick's grave was to be determined.

After his death, his body was to be placed in a cart drawn by two oxen. The oxen would be allowed to wander where they chose, and wherever they stopped, there would be the site of Patrick's grave. He was saddened to think that he would not be allowed to return to Armagh, the seat of the Church in Ireland, but he accepted Victor's announcement as the will of God.

53

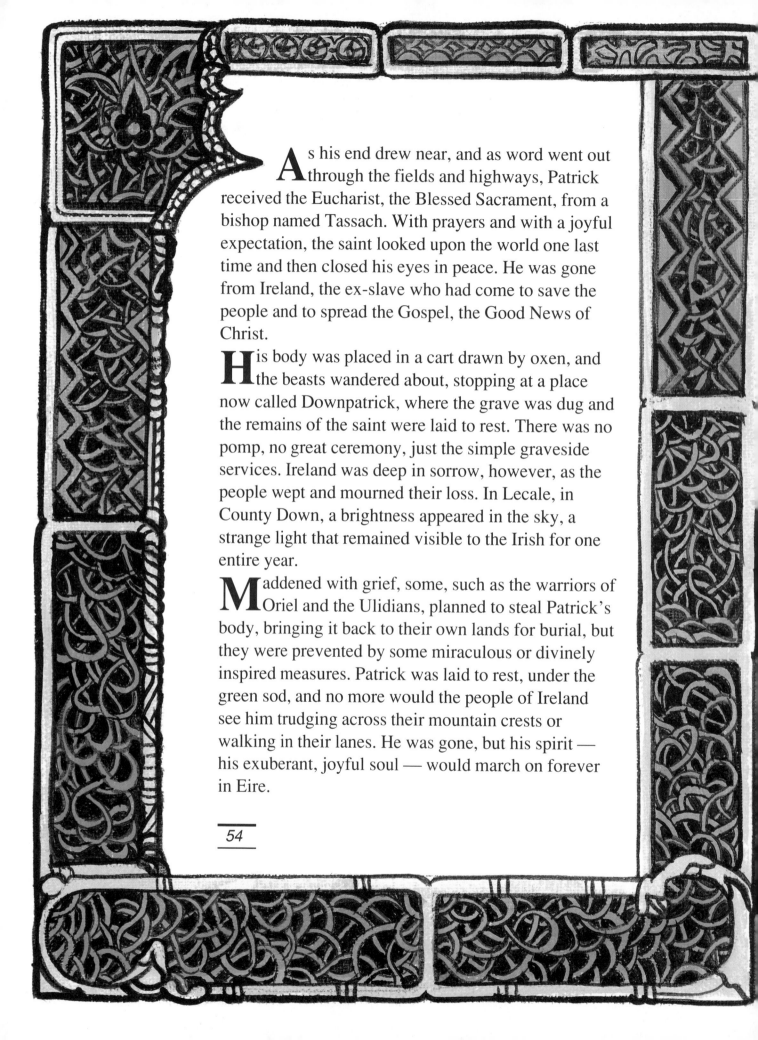

As his end drew near, and as word went out through the fields and highways, Patrick received the Eucharist, the Blessed Sacrament, from a bishop named Tassach. With prayers and with a joyful expectation, the saint looked upon the world one last time and then closed his eyes in peace. He was gone from Ireland, the ex-slave who had come to save the people and to spread the Gospel, the Good News of Christ.

His body was placed in a cart drawn by oxen, and the beasts wandered about, stopping at a place now called Downpatrick, where the grave was dug and the remains of the saint were laid to rest. There was no pomp, no great ceremony, just the simple graveside services. Ireland was deep in sorrow, however, as the people wept and mourned their loss. In Lecale, in County Down, a brightness appeared in the sky, a strange light that remained visible to the Irish for one entire year.

Maddened with grief, some, such as the warriors of Oriel and the Ulidians, planned to steal Patrick's body, bringing it back to their own lands for burial, but they were prevented by some miraculous or divinely inspired measures. Patrick was laid to rest, under the green sod, and no more would the people of Ireland see him trudging across their mountain crests or walking in their lanes. He was gone, but his spirit — his exuberant, joyful soul — would march on forever in Eire.

On March seventeenth of each year, the world looks back at Patrick. In Ireland it is a rather staid feast, which means people observe it in a quiet, dignified sort of way. The Irish must chuckle when they see how their patron is greeted in other lands and in other places. Throughout the world, in the strangest locales, including Kalakaua Avenue in Waikiki (which is part of Honolulu, Hawaii), bands march down the pavement and the sound of drums and pipes echo up into the mountains and over the sea. Wherever the story of Patrick has been heard, in fact, people of all faiths and all nationalities take time out to wear the green and to toast the patron of Erin.

Parades in Rome, Chicago, Sidney, and elsewhere are famous, none more so than the St. Patrick's Day Parade in New York City. There New York's "finest," the police, march proudly behind Patrick's banner. In other cities the Friendly Sons of St. Patrick and other fraternal groups don their hats and shamrocks and step out, often aided by Scottish bagpipers who play Irish airs for the occasion.

The first American St. Patrick's Day Parade took place in 1762, which was before America became the United States. New York City hosted that first parade and has conducted one ever since. The Irish are joined by friends and neighbors, even by total strangers, in looking back to an ex-slave who loved Ireland and its wonderful people.

THE 'BREASTPLATE' OF ST. PATRICK

Christ be with me, Christ be before me,
    Christ be behind me, Christ be in me,
Christ be beneath me, Christ be above me,
Christ be to the right of me, Christ be to the left of me,
Christ in lying down, Christ in sitting, Christ in rising up,
Christ be in the heart of everyone who may think of me,
Christ be in the mouth of everyone who may speak to me,
Christ be in every eye that may look at me,
Christ be in every ear that may hear me.